THE LIFE OF
RUBY BRIDGES

BY ELIZABETH RAUM

SEQUENCE

AMICUS | AMICUS INK

Sequence is published by Amicus and Amicus Ink
P.O. Box 227, Mankato, MN 56002
www.amicuspublishing.us

Library of Congress Cataloging-in-Publication Data
Names: Raum, Elizabeth, author.
Title: The life of Ruby Bridges / by Elizabeth Raum.
Description: Mankato, Minnesota : Amicus, [2020] | Series: Sequence change maker
  biographies | Includes index. | Audience: Grades K-3.
Identifiers: LCCN 2018031885 (print) | LCCN 2018032714 (ebook) | ISBN
  9781681517612 (pdf) | ISBN 9781681516790 (ebook) | ISBN 9781681524658 (pbk.)
Subjects: LCSH: Bridges, Ruby--Juvenile literature. | African American children--

  Louisiana--New Orleans--Biography--Juvenile literature. | African Americans--
  Louisiana--New Orleans--Biography--Juvenile literature. | New Orleans (La.)--Race
  relations--Juvenile literature. | School integration--Louisiana--New Orleans--Juvenile
  literature.
Classification: LCC F379.N59 (ebook) | LCC F379.N59 R38 2020 (print) | DDC
  379.2/63092 [B]--dc23
LC record available at https://lccn.loc.gov/2018031885

Editor: Alissa Thielges
Designer: Ciara Beitlich
Photo Researcher: Holly Young

Photo Credits: Getty/Bettmann cover, 5, 6; iStock/DONGSEON_KIM cover; Getty/Chris
Maddaloni - CQ-Roll Call Group 6; AP/RWT 8–9; AP 10, 15; Getty/Universal History
Archive - Universal Images Group 12–13; Getty/Boston Globe 16; Flickr/Ted Eytan 19;
Amistad Research Center/Alan Wieder collection 20–21; Wiki/LBJ Presidential Library
23; Rex Features/Tina Fineberg 24; Wiki/Texas A&M University-Commerce Marketing
Communications Photography 27; Alamy/American Photo Archive 28–29

TABLE OF CONTENTS

Who is Ruby Bridges?

When she was just six years old, Ruby Bridges became an American hero. She was the first black child to attend an all-white school in New Orleans. It wasn't easy. People yelled at her. They called her names. But Ruby didn't quit. Her courage changed people's hearts and minds.

Ruby's bravery inspired others to fight for equal rights.

LOADING...LOADING...LOADING...

The Russell Daily News

Segregation in Schools Is Outlawe

200 Farmers See Soil Erosion From Airplanes
Area Pilots, Planes Are Used to Inspect County Farm Land

Farm Land Values Drop 6 Per Cent

State to Comply With Decision, Fatzer Decides
Segregation to Be Ended in Schools As Soon as Possible

Four County Students To Get Ft. Hays Degrees

Supreme C... Finally M... Historic...

...wland Sees ...n Woe

The News

HIGH COURT BANS SEGREGATION IN PUBLIC SCHOOLS

A mother explains the Supreme Court's ruling to her daughter.

U.S. Supreme Court rules against segregation.

MAY 1954

LOADING...LOADING...

Living Under Segregation

In May of 1954, the **U.S. Supreme Court** ruled on a tough case. It was called Brown v. Board of Education. This ruling changed life in America. In many states, white and black children went to separate schools. This was called **segregation**. The Supreme Court said that separate schools are not equal. Schools now needed to **integrate**.

A few months later, on September 8, 1954, Ruby Nell Bridges was born. She lived in Tylertown, Mississippi. Her parents worked on a farm. So did her grandparents. When Ruby was four, her family moved to New Orleans, Louisiana. They hoped the bigger city would have better jobs and schools.

Most of New Orleans was segregated. Black and white families usually lived in different areas.

U.S. Supreme Court rules against segregation.

MAY 1954   SEPT. 8, 1954

ADING . . . LOADING . . .

Ruby Bridges is born.

All-black schools had less money for staff and supplies.

G . . . L O A D I N G . .

The New Orleans schools had been fighting **integration** since 1954. Ruby began kindergarten in an all-black school. That spring a judge ordered the schools to integrate. They had no choice. They began with five African-American first graders. Ruby was one of them. If her parents agreed, she would go to first grade at an all-white school.

White people hold signs and block the doors of outside an integrated school.

U.S. Supreme Court rules against segregation.

Ruby is chosen to attend an all-white school.

LOADING...

Ruby Bridges is born.

Ruby begins first grade.

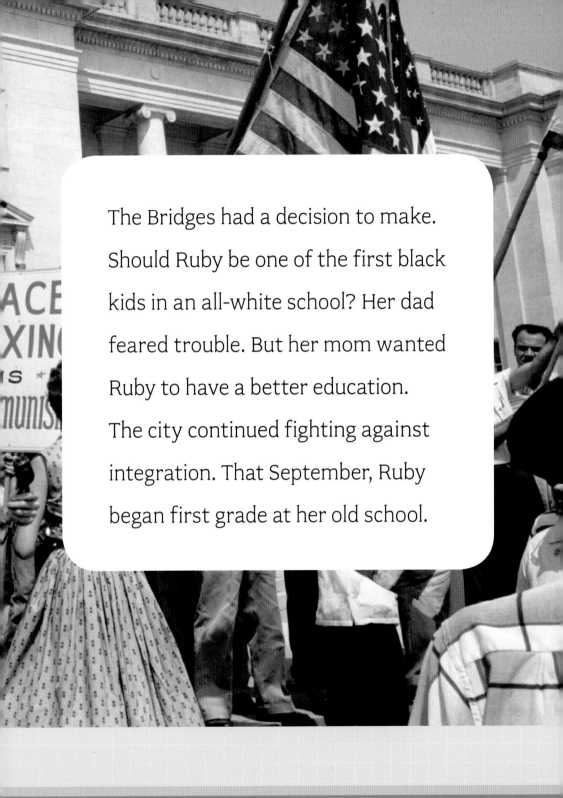

The Bridges had a decision to make. Should Ruby be one of the first black kids in an all-white school? Her dad feared trouble. But her mom wanted Ruby to have a better education. The city continued fighting against integration. That September, Ruby began first grade at her old school.

Facing Angry Crowds

On November 14, 1960, Ruby moved to the all-white school. She was the only black child going to William Franz Elementary. The other African-American first graders went to a different school. Ruby's mom went with her. So did four **federal marshals**. People were angry about integration. They took it out on Ruby. They **protested**. They yelled and threw things.

U.S. Supreme Court rules against segregation.	Ruby is chosen to attend an all-white school.	Ruby enters William Frantz Elementary.

| MAY 1954 | SEPT. 8, 1954 | SPRING 1960 | SEPT. 1960 | NOV. 14, 1960 |

Ruby Bridges is born.	Ruby begins first grade.

Federal marshals kept Ruby safe as she went to and from school.

U.S. Supreme Court rules
against segregation.

Ruby is chosen to attend an
all-white school.

Ruby enters William Frantz
Elementary.

MAY 1954　　SEPT. 8, 1954　　SPRING 1960　　SEPT. 1960　　NOV. 14, 1960　　1960–1961

Ruby Bridges is born.

Ruby begins first grade.

Ruby spends first grade as
only student in class.

Ruby did not understand why people yelled at her. Mrs. Henry, Ruby's teacher, was kind and helpful. Many people were not. Parents kept their children home from school. Ruby was the only student in her classroom. She studied alone. She ate alone. When she had to use the bathroom, a marshal walked with her to keep her safe.

Ruby's first grade teacher, Mrs. Henry, holds an old photo of her with Ruby.

Ending Segregation

Ruby felt lonely because she had no classmates. Her dad lost his job. So did her grandparents. Ruby's story was in the news. People around the country sent money and support. Slowly students returned to school. They were not in Ruby's class, but she met them. They became friends. By spring, the protesters went away.

U.S. Supreme Court rules against segregation.	Ruby is chosen to attend an all-white school.	Ruby enters William Frantz Elementary.

MAY 1954	SEPT. 8, 1954	SPRING 1960	SEPT. 1960	NOV. 14, 1960	1960–1961

Ruby Bridges is born.	Ruby begins first grade.	Ruby spends first grade as only student in class.

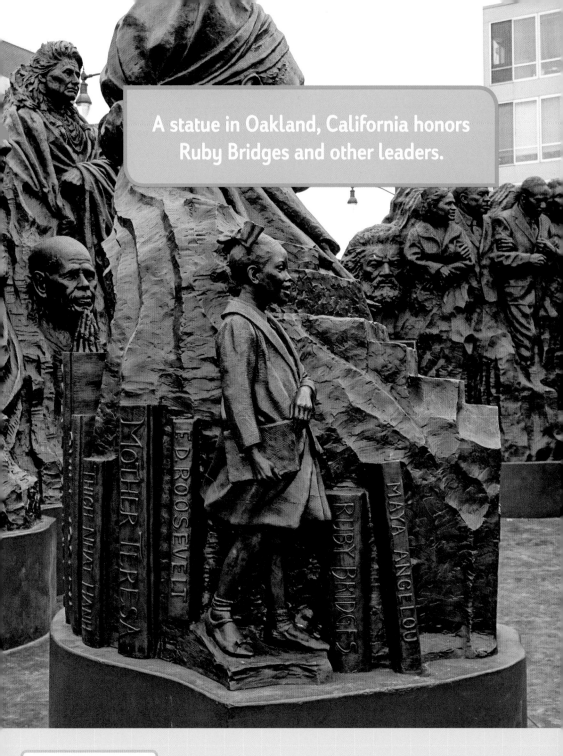

A statue in Oakland, California honors Ruby Bridges and other leaders.

U.S. Supreme Court rules against segregation.

Ruby is chosen to attend an all-white school.

Ruby enters William Frantz Elementary.

MAY 1954   SEPT. 8, 1954   SPRING 1960   SEPT. 1960   NOV. 14, 1960   1960–1961

Ruby Bridges is born.

Ruby begins first grade.

Ruby spends first grade as only student in class.

Ruby entered second grade in the fall of 1961. Other students joined her class. People stopped protesting. Ruby's bravery moved people. Norman Rockwell, a famous artist, painted a picture of Ruby. In it she walks between the federal marshals. She looks small but proud and determined. The painting was printed in *Look* magazine on January 14, 1964.

Ruby makes friends with kids in her grade.

Protests slowly end.

SPRING 1961   JAN. 1964   DING . . . LOADING . . .

Painting of Ruby is in *Look* magazine.

Equal Rights for All

On July 2, 1964, President Lyndon Johnson signed the Civil Rights Act. Ruby had just finished third grade. This act made it illegal to **discriminate** because of race, color, sex, religion, or **national origin**. There were no more all-black or all-white schools. Now all schools were integrated. **Racism** didn't end right away, but this was an important step forward.

U.S. Supreme Court rules against segregation.

Ruby is chosen to attend an all-white school.

Ruby enters William Frantz Elementary.

MAY 1954   SEPT. 8, 1954   SPRING 1960   SEPT. 1960   NOV. 14, 1960   1960–1961

Ruby Bridges is born.

Ruby begins first grade.

Ruby spends first grade as only student in class.

Reporters watch as President Johnson signs the Civil Rights Act.

Protests slowly end.

Civil Rights Act becomes law.

SPRING 1961   JAN. 1964   JULY 2, 1964   . . . LOADING . . .

Painting of Ruby is in *Look* magazine.

Ruby reads a book about her life to first graders.

U.S. Supreme Court rules against segregation.

Ruby is chosen to attend an all-white school.

Ruby enters William Frantz Elementary.

MAY 1954   SEPT. 8, 1954   SPRING 1960   SEPT. 1960   NOV. 14, 1960   1960–1961

Ruby Bridges is born.

Ruby begins first grade.

Ruby spends first grade as only student in class.

Thanks to the Civil Rights Act, Ruby went to an integrated high school in New Orleans. After high school, Ruby worked as a travel agent. In 1984, she married Malcolm Hall. They lived in New Orleans. Ruby raised four sons. When her nephews attended William Franz Elementary, Ruby volunteered there.

Protests slowly end.

Civil Rights Act becomes law.

SPRING 1961   JAN. 1964   JULY 2, 1964   1984

ADING . . .

Painting of Ruby is in *Look* magazine.

Ruby marries Malcolm Hall.

Ruby did not forget her struggle. In 1999, she wrote a children's book about her life. It is called *Through My Eyes*. She also set up The Ruby Bridges Foundation. It promotes racial **tolerance**. In 2009, she wrote another children's book, *Ruby Bridges Goes to School: My True Story*. Ruby wants to create change through education.

Ruby signs a copy of her book, *Through My Eyes.*

U.S. Supreme Court rules against segregation.

Ruby is chosen to attend an all-white school.

Ruby enters William Frantz Elementary.

MAY 1954   SEPT. 8, 1954   SPRING 1960   SEPT. 1960   NOV. 14, 1960   1960–1961

Ruby Bridges is born.

Ruby begins first grade.

Ruby spends first grade as only student in class.

Protests slowly end.

Civil Rights Act becomes law.

Ruby writes a book and sets up The Ruby Bridges Foundation.

SPRING 1961   JAN. 1964   JULY 2, 1964   1984   1999

Painting of Ruby is in *Look* magazine.

Ruby marries Malcolm Hall.

President Obama thanks Ruby for her bravery.

U.S. Supreme Court rules against segregation.		Ruby is chosen to attend an all-white school.		Ruby enters William Frantz Elementary.	
MAY 1954	SEPT. 8, 1954	SPRING 1960	SEPT. 1960	NOV. 14, 1960	1960–1961
	Ruby Bridges is born.		Ruby begins first grade.		Ruby spends first grade as only student in class.

In the summer of 2011, Norman Rockwell's painting was on display in the White House. On July 15 that year, Ruby visited President Barack Obama. He said, "If it wasn't for you guys, I wouldn't be here today." Today, Ruby talks with children about her experience. Her life proves that one child can change the world.

Protests slowly end.		Civil Rights Act becomes law.		Ruby writes a book and sets up The Ruby Bridges Foundation.	
SPRING 1961	JAN. 1964	JULY 2, 1964	1984	1999	2011
	Painting of Ruby is in *Look* magazine.		Ruby marries Malcolm Hall.		Ruby visits the White House.

Glossary

discriminate To unfairly treat a person or group different from others.

federal marshal A police officer or guard under the direction of the United States government.

integrate To bring together or combine.

integration In schools, the act of bringing together or combining students of different races in one building.

national origin The nation a person's family is originally from.

protest To object to something strongly and in public.

racism Belief that one race is better than another.

segregation The act or practice of keeping people or groups apart.

tolerance A fair or positive attitude toward those who have different beliefs, practices, or racial or ethic origins.

U.S. Supreme Court The highest court in the nation; it often makes decisions in difficult situations like civil rights.

Read More

Bridges, Ruby. *Ruby Bridges Goes To School: My True Story.* New York: Scholastic, 2009.

Harrison, Vashti. *Little Leaders: Bold Women in Black History.* New York: Little Brown and Company, 2017.

Hood, Susan. *Shaking Things Up: 14 Young Women Who Changed the World.* New York: HarperCollins, 2018.

Ribke, Simone T. *Ruby Bridges.* New York: Children's Press, 2015.

Websites

Kids Encyclopedia | Ruby Bridges
https://kids.kiddle.co/Ruby_Bridges

Ruby Bridges: A Simple Act of Faith
http://teacher.scholastic.com/activities/ruby-bridges/ruby-bridges-for-kids.htm

Index

About the Author

Elizabeth Raum has written over 100 books for young readers. Many are biographies. She enjoys learning about people who help us see the world in new and exciting ways. She lives in Fargo, North Dakota. To learn more, visit her website: www.ElizabethRaumBooks.com.